The Life I Lived With So Called
Elvis

by
Judith Martin

authorHOUSE™

1663 LIBERTY DRIVE, SUITE 200
BLOOMINGTON, INDIANA 47403
(800) 839-8640
WWW.AUTHORHOUSE.COM

This book is a work of non-fiction. Unless otherwise noted, the author and the publisher make no explicit guarantees as to the accuracy of the information contained in this book and in some cases, names of people and places have been altered to protect their privacy.

© 2005 Judith Martin. All Rights Reserved.

No part of this book may be reproduced, stored in a retrieval system, or transmitted by any means without the written permission of the author.

First published by AuthorHouse 10/21/05

ISBN: 1-4208-6641-9 (sc)

Printed in the United States of America
Bloomington, Indiana

This book is printed on acid-free paper.

Dedicated - To my grandchildren and my best friend Linda Viau.

The Life I Lived With So Called Elvis

It was a rainy Sunday night, and my two girlfriends called me to see if I would go to the Sunday night dance with them. I said I did not want to go because I was not in the mood. Margaret said, "Oh, there is no point in staying home by yourself." I said okay, and then I had to get ready. We would all meet at the hall around the same time.

I am not one to walk into a dance by myself. I feel like everyone has their eyes on me. I arrived there at 7 PM, and shortly after I arrived, Margaret and June arrived together. Then we all went inside the hall. We liked to sit on the far right side of the dance floor right by the bar. I am not a drinker. We all sat down and started talking.

I happened to look across the floor, and to my far left, I saw a man sitting as far in the corner as he could be.

I had seen this man around dances before.

I was beginning to realize that I could not keep my eyes off of him. It was because this man reminded me of Elvis Presley. His tense smile was filled with a natural grace that any beholder of snow-white teeth could love.

The highlight of his Indian heritage was in his high cheekbones as they were revealed through his adventurously dark complexion. As I picked up all my benevolent features more strongly, my heart was beginning to race and burn in the extreme.

My mind was suddenly turning into to a melodramatic hurricane as I glanced toward the entrance. There he was making his way through the crowd and talking up a storm by the electricity it produced. Everything seemed to embellish even more of his mystery—like his black jeans; his long, black-sleeved, cotton shirt; and black corduroy jacket. He seemed to be untouched from the outside.

As Mother Nature's force of the rain began its own dance with the wind, my pretentious Elvis, yet untouched like any other man, moved his body of ambiguity toward the bar for a good old bottle of beer. That electricity of his was making the pores all over my skin electrocute me, which only stimulating love at first sight could produce.

Perhaps he would be like a blatant romantic and ask me to dance one song. He never did. Instead, my man of mystery, my pretentious Elvis, decided to go sit down at his table in the mysterious corner.

But at least it was within reach of my table. He sat there as if he were a statue of greatness only to be viewed from afar. Once again he began to move. My heart was not only racing with itself but was beginning to race with the very air that filled the dance hall.

Creating what I could feel as with a heat of anticipation In to a question: Will he ask me to dance? I was still intrigued with this man. My thoughts were racing. They were playing an Elvis song called "Can't Help Falling in Love." Then I saw this man get up, and he started to walk across the floor toward our table. I felt excited, thinking he would ask me to dance. But instead, with his terribly angular-poised posture, he leaned over to my girlfriend Margaret. She knew better than to take up his offer and simply said no to my mystery man.

The First Time I Met Elvis

Suddenly this haunting Elvis asked me to dance. Oh God, he had just picked me as his second choice for the evening. I leaped off my chair better than any frog in the universe and said yes with a bunch of air caught in my throat.

"My name is Don. What is yours?"

Plain and simple, I breathlessly replied, "Judith." At the end of that song, Don said he liked dancing. Now I knew his name was Don, so we danced and talked as we danced.

I was thinking he was a strange person who loved to dance and not stop, and I was having a good time. I was wearing a pink fitted dress with a gold belt ¾ inches wide. I was five feet seven, with sandy-blond, shoulder-length hair and hazel eyes. And by this time of night he would dance his way and I would dance mine. Slow ones were not so bad that a little practice wouldn't fix them, so now my mind was saying that I was glad that he asked me to dance.

I had gotten such a rush from Don. I don't know why right now. But now it was time to leave the dance.

The Life I Lived With So Called Elvis

Don asked me if he could take me home. It made me feel good, but I said, "No, I don't know you, so I would not go by myself."

So he gave me his phone number. He told me, "If you call me, you call ... If you don't, you don't."

This was a Sunday night, September 2nd, and I felt good about it, but I found it too much of a challenge, a rush. So then I said, "Thanks for the dances."

So then I went home, and when I got there, Don was on my mind. I was asking myself if I should see him, but the voice in my head said, "Go for it. What do I have to lose?" So this was Monday, September 3rd, and I still could not make up my mind whether I could make that phone call to Don.

Now it was Monday night. Thinking about it made me fluttery inside. I tried to watch TV but could not keep my mind on it. I tried to read. Then it was time to go to bed. But because of the excitement, it was hard for me to fall asleep. Now it was Tuesday. I got up thinking about Don and my heart was still going patter-patter, and now it was about 5:30 PM.

I still could not make my mind up to make that phone call. I did make that call. Don said, "Hello."

I said, "Hello. This is Judith from the dance. Do you remember me?"

Don said, "Yes, I do." I was very nervous because I am old fashioned. That did not make things easy, so Don said, "How are you? I didn't think you would call." Don went on to ask me if I would like to meet him at Tim Horton after he went to the show because he had already made plans.

So I was very excited. I don't know why it never bothered me before to do this. I said okay. Don said, "How about 9 PM?"

Now all I could think about was the first dance. The song was "Can't Help Falling in Love," and of course they played a few other Elvis songs like "Are You Lonesome Tonight," "Blue Hawaii," and "G.I. Blues." On our first date, we went out to Tim Horton's for tea. We talked for about two hours. Don talked about his daughter, who was going to go to law school.

Don told me that she was eighteen, and as he was talking, I was trying to find out in my mind how old Don was. But he was not old enough to have a daughter that old. So I let him go on and on. Don said that she looked a lot like him. She had long black hair, deep brown eyes, and was as tall as he was. Also that she was a bleeder. Then I asked Don, "Do you have any more children?" His answer was NO. Then Don started to talk about his mom, and he said that she was in her seventies and lived by herself.

Don told me she had a heart condition, and I said, "Is she all right to be on her own?" Don said yes. I told Don that I was a medical assistant and that if she needed help with anything, I could give her hand.

Don said, "That would be nice of you. Thank you for offering your help." At this point, I still had not given Don my phone number. He asked me if I would like to go dancing on Friday evening. I accepted. As we talked, Don was a happy camper with a smile on his face all the time. I don't know if this was good or bad; how many men smile a lot?

The Life I Lived With So Called Elvis

Still I did not give Don my phone number, as I didn't know him at all. I would see how it went on Friday night. We were going to a country and western dance. I don't mind country dancing as long as I am dancing. Well, it was Friday night, and I met him at the dance hall at 8:30 PM. The band did not start until 9. Here we go again talking about his life. He told me he was not married but had a daughter who was going to a university to be a doctor.

Don must have forgotten what he had told me on Tuesday night. I started thinking about this man—he told me one thing one day and then forgot what he had told me the next time. Well, I didn't know about him. I thought I would give him a chance until I found out differently. Now the band started and off we went to dance. Don was no dancer, but to each his own. Don did the same step to everything. During Don's fast ones, I had to laugh to myself as all kinds of things were going through my head. Out of the blue, he asked me, "Would you like to go dancing on Saturday night? We could go to someplace you like to go."

I thought to myself, "I am a ballroom dancer, but I do like any kind of music. I can dance to anything; there is nothing I can't do when it comes to dancing." So I said okay. I am a fool for someone who is different; people can be cruel when it comes to someone who is different.

Don could not do ballroom dancing because he got his body going in one direction and his arms in the other, and when I danced slowly he just stood in one spot, and when I did ballroom dancing, I was moving like a bird gliding across the floor, moving quite fast, but who was I if I didn't give Don a chance to try, right? So after the dance, I let him bring me home, and then I invited Don

Judith Martin

in for a tea. He was quite the gentle man. He had tea, and I told Don it was getting late, and off he went. But first, he asked me out for Saturday night to go dancing, and I said yes. I thought that if we danced for a few weeks just maybe he would catch on.

This time he had too much to drink, so I said, "You may sleep on my couch." Things were going great except when it came to the weekend. Don left and told me he would be back in two hours. I asked him where he was going. He said he had to go do his hair. I said to him, "Well, you could do it here."

"No," he said to me, "it has to be done in a cold room."

I turned to him and said, "I don't know what you're talking about."

Don said he puts his air conditioning on. I thought this was rather strange but said nothing. He was very much a gentleman and would use his manners like "please," "thank you," and "you're welcome." Then came Friday again, and we went to the Leander Boat Club. We had a great time. This guy had dancing on his mind 24-7, and I didn't mind because I could dance around the clock. Don asked me if I would like to do something on Sunday. Guess what. Yes, you guessed it—we went dancing again. I don't mind because I love it.

I began to notice that every time we went out, he drank. It was not a lot so I did not think too much about it. He started to talk to me more about his life. He told me he owned a big house. That did not matter to me at this point.

We continued to see each other and had now been going out for two months. I still had not seen his house.

The Life I Lived With So Called Elvis

Don never asked me to go see his place. I found this to be strange. I was not sure if I should keep going out with him or not. I was finding that some things he was doing and saying were scary, but I kept telling myself that things would get better. So far all I had done with Don was go dancing.

Now six months had gone by, and still I hadn't seen his place. He told me it was a big mansion on the mountain. I said I would like to see it on Saturday. Don said nothing when it came to Saturday. I reminded him he promised to take me to the house, but he had an excuse. "You have excuses all the time for something," I told Don. "If I do not see this house, everything between us is over."

After all this, we went and saw this big house. He stood there and said to me, "What you see is not what you see." So, I think most men when they are caught doing things or saying things that are not true. I was not so stupid as to fall for this statement. It was like when they are caught in bed with someone, the first thing out of their mouths is, "This is not what it looks like."

I found this statement hard to handle. I was thinking, "There is something not right about this situation." I then said to him, "What is that supposed to mean?" He told me he lived in one room and rented out the rest. I could not see anybody who owned a home like that just occupying one room. Somehow I didn't believe this. Don asked me to just wait there; he would be right back. I started asking myself, "What the hell is going on here?" Then back he came and said okay. So we went inside and upstairs to his one room. In that one room he had a small fridge, small table, TV, sofa, oh and a telephone. Then he said that there was a man who lived upstairs from him and downstairs lived a husband and wife. I have to tell you, I was never so shocked in my life. .

For a man who works for the city, he made big bucks. Not knowing what to say, no words came out of my mouth. Fishy? I thought so.

We left, and we went on like things where okay. Still I was trying to figure out how he could think I would fall for this. He had another thing coming. We went back to my place just like nothing happened.

So I asked Don if he would mind leaving early, thinking I had my job cut out for me now. So by now, I figured I had heard all lies in the last six months, and I started to do some checking. At one time I was a private investigator, so I went to work and soon found out it was not his house and that he was just renting a room in it, that's all.

First Breakup

I just did not want to see him again, and I told Don that. All he did was keep calling me and leaving messages on my answering machine and singing "Are You Lonesome Tonight?" over and over till my machine was full. The next day, he started sending flowers and cards to my door.

I did not see him after this for about two weeks. It was very hard since I loved him. After all these lies, he called me again and said he was so sorry. I said, "That does not make it any easier." Don asked me if I would like to meet his daughter; her name was Lori. He wanted me to meet him at Limeridge Mall, and there I could meet Lori. I said I would.

The First Time I Met His Daughter

This was a Saturday afternoon around 3 PM. We met in the food court. First I saw Don coming, then right beside him was his daughter. I could tell that Don was the father; they looked so much alike. She did look well-dressed, with beautiful, long, black hair and a lot of it. She was a daddy's girl. Don said, "Lori, this is Judith."

Lori said, "Hi, nice to meet you." We all had some lunch and talked for a bit. Lori seemed to like me straight away. Lori was very pretty. Lori asked me if she could have my phone number. Her dad said no, and Lori got upset. But I slipped it to her under the table anyway.

Shortly after her dad had dropped her off at home, my phone rang, and it was Lori. We talked for some time. Lori told me her dad did not want her to know where I lived. I asked Lori, "How old are you?" Lori said she was fourteen—too young to be in a university, also too young to even think of being a doctor. My suspicions were beginning to come true.

I asked Lori, "May I have your phone number?"

The Life I Lived With So Called Elvis

She said, "Yes, but don't let my dad know." I said okay. I let things pass for a while. When it came to Sunday again, he told me he wanted to see Lori so he left. I got a phone call from Don saying he was dropping Lori off at his mother's and would be right over.

His mother only lived twenty minutes away. An hour and a half went by and no Don. At this point, I decided to call his mother since I was getting worried. So I called, and she asked, "Who are you?" I told her I was Don's girlfriend. She was shocked. She told me he was married with two girls, one seven and the other fourteen, which was Lori. She also told me he had another girl with another woman. Well, I was dumfounded by this news.

Don's mother also told me that he did not support these children. Well, you can imagine where my mind went. It seemed like all he did was tell lies right, left, and center.

Let me tell you, my heart was racing 90 miles an hour. I said to myself, "Do I want to see this deranged man?" I am telling you, I sat and cried like a big baby. My whole insides were upside down. I wanted to really destroy him without batting an eye in the worst way. Unless you are in my shoes you would not know what you would do but when you fall in love, you are sometimes so stupid about it all.

Finally Don arrived at my place. I asked him where he had been. He told me he had been at his mother's. I told him he was lying, and an argument started, and this time I yelled at him to leave, but he started lying, and I could not stand people who lied to me.

First I told Don that I called his mother. Don said, "Why did you do that?"

I said, "You told me that you would drop Lori off and be right here, and it would have taken you fifteen minutes to come from there. Where did you go from there?" He told me he was at his mother's, but I found out he stopped at his wife's. I told him, "Don, I know where you went," and Don said he did not. But Don's mother had told me that was where he went. I could not tell him that she told me this because she was afraid of him, and I told her I wouldn't.

So after we finished arguing, I told him to leave, and I slammed the door in his face.

The next day—can you believe it?—Don had the nerve to call me again. I told him I was going to see his wife. He then told me she would beat the shit out of me. I told him, "Don, if I am not afraid of you, I am sure not going to be afraid of your wife." I found this to be hilarious. He did not think I would do such a thing. I proved him wrong when I went over the next day to speak with his wife.

She answered the door. I told her my name, and she said, "Come in."

I told her about what Don had told me. "If I came to see you, you would beat the shit out of me." She told me that I was not the first woman that had come to her. We sat and I had tea. We talked and she told me everything, like ever since they were married, he would take off every Saturday and Sunday night and would come home on Monday after work or whenever he wanted to.

I asked her, "Why do you put up with this?"

She replied, "Because I love him, and I am afraid because he pushed me around and he had pushed me down the stairs. So whatever he does or tells me to do I do it."

The Life I Lived With So Called Elvis

I told her she had rights and could have a peace bond on him to keep him away. She said, "No way." She let him come and go, and she would take his clothes to wash.

Then I said to myself, "There is a way I can put a stop to this."

But it would take some time. This meant I would have to spend time with the animal until it was completed. To look at her and see how afraid she was made me determined to do something for her. Now, you can call me crazy. What I had in mind would take some time, so as the story goes on, I will fill you in.

I had met all three girls, and they were afraid of their dad too. The young one sat on my lap the whole time I was there. Don's wife showed me through her house. She showed me all the love letters he wrote to her just to keep her hanging on. Her walls had pictures of him everywhere. Then I was in her bedroom, and I saw things that I had given to Don and asked her where she got those things. She told me, "Don." I told her that I had given those to Don and wondered why he wanted to take them to work to show the men he worked with. In my mind, I didn't think men did things like that. So he took them, and this was where they ended up, so she gave them back to me. I felt bad, and I don't have to tell you how mad I was about it all and what she was going through.

I told her that I had better go because it was late. She asked me if she could come to my place and stay the night. I said, "Most certainly." So she came over and brought the two girls, and then Lori came over later, and we did a lot of talking. The mother looked dragged out. Her hair was a mess, so I gave her a perm because I am a hairdresser and had all that stuff on hand. I put the kids to bed at about 2 AM. She was happy because someone cared about her.

After I finished doing her hair and had tea, it was about 5 AM. We went to bed for what was left of the morning. I got up at about eight o'clock and made the breakfast. Then I took them all home. She wanted me to go in with her, so I did. While she was gone, Don had come to her home and pulled the phone out of the wall and ripped all the drapes off the windows and threw a few things around the house, so I told her to call the police.

But she said it would make things worse for her. I told her, "If you let him know that you are afraid of him, then he will keep doing it to you." She said I would pay dearly. Well, we were not in the house too long before he called her and wanted to know where she was. He was giving her a hard time. Then she told him that she stayed at my place all night and he was hot under the collar said a few harsh words to her and hung up. She had to let go. I said, "Thanks and don't worry, but if Don does anything to you, feel free to call me, and I will put a stop to it." Well, I knew I would hear from him, and sure enough, he called, and I asked if he was coming over. He said yes, and I just played it cool and let him come over. We sat a bit then I told him I knew the truth now, and I said to him, "Do you want to tell me where you really were?" In doing this, he really got mad. He got up from the sofa and tried to leave because he was caught in another lie. So I grabbed him right by the shirt on each side of his neck, and I literally picked Don up and threw him ass over tea kettle right over the sofa.

The Life I Lived With So Called Elvis

This was the shock of his life. Don got up and said, "Don't you ever do that again."

I said, "Then don't you give me a reason to do so." I told him to sit down till I was finished talking and then he could go. So we talked about what he did to his wife and kids. I asked Don, "Why are you not supporting your kids and wife?" Don said that she had a boyfriend.

I told him that she told me he would not let her. He said, "That's not true."

Of course I was on her side. I could not believe him at this point at all, and while I was at it, I also told him, "If you ever hurt your mother, you will have me to deal with, and the next time it will be worse than what I just did to you." So after we finished, Don left in a fit.

Well, I was beginning to think, "What did I get myself into with the Elvis?" but when you fall in love with someone and you are in deep, it is. So there I was stuck in love with this so-called Elvis, the pretender. Don was good looking, like Elvis, tall, athletic, and loved to run. He told me he was in martial arts and boxing. If that were the case, I would not have flipped him so easily. On the other hand, I had been doing kung fu and kickboxing for years.

But this is one thing you do not go around telling people because if I am with some guy and he wants to get smart, he will soon find out that it will soon be over and he will leave with his tail between his legs. I am telling you, as you could imagine, Don left, and I did not hear from him for a couple of days.

Then he called and said he wanted me to cool down. Don said, "I have never seen so much hate in any woman's eyes like I saw in yours." I told him I had every reason to have that hate in my eyes.

Then it came to Friday, and Don phoned and said he had to do something, but he would not tell me what. I jumped in my car and went to his place. His car was parked out in front. I was singing "One Broken Heart for Sale." I knew he was not out. I went and knocked on the door. He did not answer the door. The next day, he called, and I started to see him again. After work, he would go home, shower, and change, then come over. He seemed always to have some excuse to leave. It was starting to affect my nerves. Now I was crying in the chapel then drying my eyes. Then I started to follow him and found out that he was going to his wife's house for her to do his hair, to dye it jet black. I found this out from Don's mother, and I asked her, "What do you mean he goes there every time to dye his hair?"

When I saw him, I put it to him once again, and as you know, he denied it. But he did not know that I followed him. It was one winter night, and I decided to follow him again. I waited for him. I saw him coming, and then I cut him off at the mall. Well, he started to hide his car. When Don saw me, he took off like lightning. He called me the next day.

I told him I was going away to be a nun as I had talked about before. As I mentioned before, I would fix him for what he did to his wife and kids.

So I would put up with this until I did it my way. I had to keep my mind clear so the best thing to do was to move. I called Don and told him I was leaving to become a nun and that I would write him or call if I was ever in

The Life I Lived With So Called Elvis

Hamilton for a meeting. About three weeks had gone by and I was in Hamilton, so I called Don at work.

I asked if I could speak to Don please, and then he came to the phone, and he sounded choked because it was me. He asked if I would like to meet him for lunch. Well, you know the answer to that, I am sure. We met and we talked about why I wanted to be a nun because I think nuns are like angels and that that was my calling and I missed it. Don asked me, "How long do you have to make up your mind if you are staying or getting out?"

I said there was a three months' grace. If I wanted out, I had to do it at the end of the three months.

So I hope you can read between the lines about the nun part. Don told me he was not going out dancing; he was staying in. If I believed that I was a bigger fool than he was. I knew for sure he met a lady and he was taking her out on Sunday night but not where I met him. This dance was out of town. One of my friends saw him and told me, so I had to see it to believe it—not that I cared.

Trusting someone is the key to having a good relationship.

Now Sunday night came, and I thought I would go there and see for myself. I don't know why I did this, but having been a private investigator, I had to find out just what was going on. So now I was at the dance hall, and as soon as I walked in, someone that knew Don and I had been going out for some time came up to me and said, "Do you want to meet the girl that Don was seeing when you were away?"

I said, "Not really."

But this guy said, "There she is, across the other side of the room." So he just took my arm and pulled me over there.

I spoke to the lady, and she said, "You must be Don's girlfriend."

I said I was.

"Well," she said, "this guy is out of his mind. He keeps calling, and I will not tell you the words." All of a sudden, I saw him enter the hall, and I headed to the back of the hall and in behind the curtains on the stage.

I could see him walking up one side then down the other. Don started to ask girls to dance, and he was turned down every time. This time he had passed by me and did not see me. He was with a screwball guy. I did not like this man at all or trust him as far as I could throw him. He had sneaky-looking eyes.

Now I thought I would come out of hiding. It did not take Don too long to find me sitting at a table. Don came over, and I told him to get lost. Don said to me, "I love you."

I said, "No, you don't."

Don said, "I will be back in a minute. I have something for you in my car."

"I don't want anything from you." He left, and in five minutes, he was back with a rose. I told him, "I don't want nothing from you. Go give it to the girl across the room."

Don said, "I don't know anyone over there." I asked him if he was seeing a lady from here. He said, "Don't be so silly. I love you."

So again I told him to get lost. He said, "Let's dance and I will leave you alone." So I did dance with him, then

The Life I Lived With So Called Elvis

I told him to stay away from me. Before he left, he said, "Yes, I took her out for a coffee." I said that she told me he kept calling her. Well, again he apologized, and I took him back. I know what you are thinking, but hold on. If you remember what I said throughout the book, you know why I took him back for the umpteenth time.

As the saying goes, love is blind. Don started to come over for dinner. It got so that he was coming over every night, seven days a week. In all that time, all he brought was a bottle of wine for our candlelight dinner. I finally said to him, "Look here, enough of this bullshit. I am paying for everything here. It is about time you shell out, so if you want to eat here, then you buy and I'll cook."

Don said he would buy the food. After that, he started to take me out once in a while to the Swiss chalet when he came over to see me at night. Don would bring me flowers and cards. Not too many men do that. I started to wonder what he was up to. More and more flowers came and were put at my door. After an examination of these, I realized there were wooden sticks in them. Then I started to realize that the only time sticks are put in flowers are when they are for a funeral, not if you go in and buy flowers.

Then I realized Don worked at the cemetery and made eighteen dollars an hour. He had lots of money, but he did not mind spending it on booze.

This was going on, and I found out that Don was an alcoholic, but a good one because you could not smell it on him at any time, no matter how much he would drink.

He would stay the same, never change this manner.

The Life I Lived With So Called Elvis

When he would drink too much, he would ask if he could stay the night. I said yes, and this was why he would like me to take my car. Then Don started staying over on weekends, but the rest of the week he was over every night. Then he would go home and call me. We would talk for about two hours, and things started to go okay. I told him it was her or me. After a year of this, I started to smarten up.

Now it was close to Christmas. I did not see him Christmas Day because he wanted to see his kids, and I thought that was okay so he came over later. He brought me a sweater and a phone. He said to me, "I'll bet nobody else has bought you nice gifts like these."

I just laughed to myself. He thought he was the best man there was out there, saying things like that. You know where that came from. Thinking that he was Elvis. I noticed that when we were out, Don thought that because he looked like Elvis that the women were looking at him. As strange as this may seem, I am not an Elvis fan. I like his music, but I am not a collector of Elvis things.

The longer I knew Don, the more I saw that he thought he was Elvis. After I found out that he was still coloring his hair, I told Don, "If you think you are sleeping on my pillows, you are not."

Don asked, "How did you know I color my hair?"

I told him, "I am a hairdresser."

I know when someone colors his or her hair. So he stopped, and then you could see the gray coming through. I asked Don to bring the height of his hair down, so he said okay. So then it looked better. No one has ever seen me with a wet head, and I said, "What makes you different after a few weeks?" Don started letting me do his hair

Judith Martin

in a cold room because if it was hot, his hair would not do what he wanted it to. I laughed to myself. I thought that Don was from another planet.

Don was a very jealous man. He did not like it if I spoke to another man. He went right into orbit. This was the first part of January, and all the gentleman said was "Happy New Year." Don was so boisterous and said all kinds of things like "Did you go out with him?" "Did you sleep with him?" and so on.

I was so embarrassed that I wanted to throw him ass over tea kettle from his seat. I knew that if I hit him I would end up in jail for assault, so I told him, "If you ever do that to me again, I will have you banned from this dance."

Don said, "You can't do that."

I said, "Watch me."

He soon calmed down, then we stayed for one hour and left. A lot of things went through my mind that night. As far as I was concerned, I was still single and going to single dances. I had free will, and I had been single for twenty years. When going to these dances, you get to know a lot of men and women, and no one will tell me who I can and cannot speak to ever.

I am my own boss. I cannot understand how women can let a man tell them what to do. Every person has a mind of his or her own. If you are afraid of a man, then you should not be with him. Move on. There are more fish in the sea.

But good men are hard to find. I know a lot of men who will ask you if you would like to go out for dinner, and when you say yes, then they think you are their dessert, and there are so many women that are taken in

The Life I Lived With So Called Elvis

by this. Well, if you want to put a stop to getting manhandled, and they think you are their dessert.

What I do is when I am asked out for dinner, I come right out and tell the man, "If you think that I am your dessert, then forget it." This will weed them out really fast. I also tell the man I am not a one-night stand for any man.

A woman has to have standards to live by. I think every woman should take the basics of kung fu. This is a very fast move, and you should get them before they get you. The sooner you learn this, the sooner you will feel a lot better about yourself and keep it to yourself. The fewer people who know, the better off you are. Trust me, I have taken out a few with one move.

This will also make you stronger, and fitness kickboxing is one fantastic workout. But I must tell you, it is addictive but well worth it. It makes you feel good and look good, and gives you a good complexion. But then you have to remember if you take these courses, you are not allowed to hit anyone first. Let them hit you first, then this is called self-defense.

So I advise all women to please take some kind of self-defense course. Well, this is enough of this, so now let's talk about New Year's Eve. As I said in the first part of the book, Don liked to dress in black all the time. I asked Don nicely, "Please, would you dress up nice?"

Don said yes, but I was still wearing my black suit jacket. "I hope you will wear a pink shirt," he said, "if you can find one." We were off to the Amity. We went, and we did find a pink shirt.

When Don wore different clothes, he looked so good, so when Don picked me up, I said, "You look nice." It was unbelievable, and of course a lot of my friends were at the dance, and they told Don how nice he looked. He would look at people and smile, and I could see that he felt good. We all had a good time, rang in the New Year, had a bite to eat, and then went home. That was the first time I enjoyed my evening out. Things were not too bad so far. I had been with Don since 1991.

Now it was the summer of 1992. I felt I'd had enough, so I told Don to get out of my life for good. He still kept coming to my house and ringing my doorbell. I opened the door and let him in. "What the hell kind of game are you playing?" Don had been harassing me since 1991. He was told to leave me alone. Every time I told him to leave me alone and that I did not want to see him, he did damage to my car. Don put sugar in the tank of my van and put four holes in the radiator.

This was about 3 AM. Don was the one who did it. The next day, my neighbor said he saw that it was Don. But as the saying goes, if you don't see them doing it, you are out of luck. There was no need to call the police, so I let it go. The flowers and cards kept coming anyway. I did not see Don. A few weeks later, Don called again. I don't have to tell you what I did. As soon as I talked to Don, it everything started up again. I did it again. Yes, I went back to him again. Then things started. We would start running and walking at night for hours. I was working out a lot by myself. Don did not know about it. I had to keep in shape because you never know when a woman needs it. At first Don did not think I could run that far.

Don was telling me he was a black belt. That was a crock because if he was a black belt, he should have been able to stop me from flipping him. I think every woman

The Life I Lived With So Called Elvis

should have some kind of kickboxing or martial arts. You will say you don't have time. Make time. An hour out of your week or two just may save your life.

The most important thing is do not go around telling people you have this because there would be someone who would push you into using it just to see if you are or not. Remember, silence is golden. Back to my pretender Elvis. With all the money he had, he was cheap.

If we went to a show, it had to be on a Tuesday night because that was two-dollar night, but when it came to his drinking, it did not matter what he spent. Well, now it was getting on to Christmas again, and it had been a long time since my ex and I separated, but we had agreed that we would have Christmas dinner together as a family. Don did not like it at all, so I called it off that year. On Christmas morning, Don called and told me that he had to take his kids. I said okay, and Don said that he would not be long. I found out later that he went to his wife's for Christmas dinner. Then all hell broke loose. I talked to his wife, and she told me he was there although they were separated. He still would make up lies to go over there. I also was very friendly with his wife and mother, who was seventy-seven years old. Now I was very angry at Don because I had told my ex that we could not have Christmas dinner together, so my kids had no father to spend their Christmas with. So then I called my ex and told him it was fine if he wanted to come and have dinner the next day. So everything worked out just fine. I told myself I would never ever put my kids behind any man ever. This is the worst thing you could do to your kids. I could have lost the respect of my kids. Now, as for Don's mother, she would come over sometimes for tea, or

Judith Martin

I would go there. Don did not like the idea of me being friendly with his mother because she would tell me many things that went on. His mother said he would call his ex-wife as many as fifteen times a day. I confronted him once again with this, and he said, "I love you so much. I don't want to lose you."

I told him that if we were going to be a couple, there were rules I wanted him to follow. We were to start going to church and start his divorce proceedings. I also wanted him to stop drinking. Well, he did all this for a while, and I found out from his wife that he had asked her to get started on the divorce proceedings so that her mother's allowance would pay for it and he would not have to pay for it out of his pocket. So she told me that it was started. In the meantime, Don brought me divorce papers. "Here it is, so you can look at it, and I do not want to hear about it again, and you had better change your attitude."

I looked at it, and I said, "Who do you think you are kidding? This is not even a legal document. Well, Don, when you try to trick someone, do it to someone who does not work in this field."

After Don left that night, I called his wife and asked what was going on, and she told me that Don had told her to cancel the divorce, and she had done so. The next day, I saw him. My words were, "If you do not get that divorce soon, you will find out that you will be out of my life forever, and I mean it." I started to go back to dances, and he would follow me. Love is so blind that I couldn't see the trees for the forest. One day, his daughter came to visit, and he was at my place. I told Don it was his daughter and ex-wife. Don said to not let them in. I

The Life I Lived With So Called Elvis

told him, "This is my place, and I will let in who I want to let in," and so then a fight started. Then Don tried to take his trophy from my wall unit, but we grabbed it at the same time. I told him that he had given it to me so he was not taking it. "If you do not let go, I will break it." So we struggled until it was broken, and all this time, his wife and daughter were watching, but this did not bother me. If they did not like it, they could leave. So then I threw him right into the wall. He then came back and pushed me and hurt my arm. His daughter called the police. They came but did not want to do much about it. Don's ex-wife told the police that if I would have given the trophy to him, this would not have happened.

I told her that I did not take any shit from anyone, big or small. I stand up for myself. "If you jump when he says jump, that's up to you." Don had fled when the police were called. The police found it funny that his ex-wife was at my place, so his wife left and said that it was my fault. His daughter stayed to see if her dad would come back. She waited for some time. I told her that he would not come back tonight, so I took her home and told her that if she needed me to call me and I would be right there. All this took place on a Saturday night. When Monday came, I went down to the police station and filed a complaint. He had to go to court for that. He got his ex-wife and daughter to lie for him. As the old saying goes, blood is thicker than water. There was a peace bond put on him for a year. Don would still leave notes and flowers, and go to the dances I went to. I know the people that ran the dances, and I had him barred from all of them. I told Don I would have him barred, but he did not think that I would do it. Well, think again. He

Judith Martin

still kept calling from phone booths, and when I was not home, he would call and sing the great song "Are You Lonesome Tonight?" Don sang it until the tape on the answering machine was full. I don't know what the matter was with me, but I took him back for the fifteenth time. I told him that this would be the last time I helped him. If he drank too much and lied to me, he would have to get out of my life. We tried to be just friends, but I was too concerned about what he was doing with his life. He did not drink for a month. He finally admitted to me that he was an alcoholic and needed help. So finally I took Don to see a psychiatrist. After two years of this, I gave up. After that, he would go out and look for my car. Don and his so-called friend were at a dance. I was at it with a friend, and he watched me the entire time he was there. Then I saw him and his friend starting to leave when I was dancing. I watched them both put beer bottles in their pockets and glasses up their sleeves so I followed them. He broke the side mirror of my car and put beer bottles and glasses under my tires. But having been a private investigator, I never get into my car unless I check it out first. I realized that he would never leave me alone. This happened in 1994. When Larry and I were at a dance, Don came in with his friend, and they were drinking. Don saw me and a girlfriend so he asked her to dance and she did. As I was dancing with my fiancé, Don was going in and out of the dance hall. The third time, Don and his friend took beer bottles and glasses out of the dance hall. So I told Larry that after this dance we had better get out of there because my car was right outside of the dance hall in front. I found the side mirror was kicked off, and there were beer bottles and glasses under

The Life I Lived With So Called Elvis

my tires. So I was very upset about it, and I picked up the bottles very carefully and put them in a bag and decided to take them to the police station. As I was driving down the street, I saw a police car across the street so I flagged him down. He asked me what was going on, and I told him that I was at the dance around the corner and that Don had put these bottles and glasses under my tires and I would like to have them fingerprinted. The policeman said that it was raining, and we wouldn't get anything. I asked him to please try because I had a peace bond on him. So he said okay but it would take about two weeks. I said that was okay. It took one week, and they called me and said that they had gotten a fingerprint from one of the bottles, and needless to say, off we went to court. Can you imagine that he was on probation at the age of forty-seven? He was not to be on the street after midnight and could not drink. I laughed to myself so hard and told the police officer that he would stay out as late as he wanted to. The police officer said that they knew where he went and that they would pick him up if he did. Two weeks later, the officer called me and told me that they picked him up and he spent time in jail for it. The best thing was that they arrested him at work. Then to top it all off, he had his daughter call me and ask me if I was married yet. I said, "Not yet," and she asked if I would give her dad another chance. He said that he would buy me a house and I could pick it out and that he would give in to all of my demands if I gave him another chance. I said, "No, I have given him fifteen chances, and that was already too many." It was now November 1996, and I had run into him twice. I asked him if he was singing "Jailhouse Rock" or "In the Ghetto." When I looked at him, he looked the

Judith Martin

other way. I told him that I thought of him a lot and I still loved the cards and letters that he sent me from 1991 to 1993. He had still not gotten a divorce, so I took it upon myself to go back to him on the condition that he get a divorce. Right away he said okay, but if he got the divorce, I had better straighten out. I said okay to this. So sure enough, he got his ex-wife to get the divorce through her mother's allowance so he would not have to pay for it. His wife called me and said that he really went through with it this time. I told her that now she was free from him and could get on with her life. So he brought the papers and showed me that he had gotten the divorce. I put up with him for two weeks, and then I told him to get out and that I didn't want to see him ever again. I thought that I did his wife a good deed. Now it was a year later, and I had gotten married. My husband and I went to a bar and who did I run into but Don. His daughter came up to me and gave me a big hug and said that it was nice to see me. My husband and I were playing pool. Don was watching me every chance he got, and he finally got the nerve to come up by the pool table. He just stood there and watched me until I asked him how he was. He just glared at me and went back to sit down at his table with his girlfriend and continued to watch me. He got the nerve to come up to me again and said that he thought that I had better leave. I told him that I didn't think so. I was not afraid of him before, and I was sure as hell not afraid of him now. So he went and sat down, but then he came up again and got in my face and said, "Are you married to this man?"

I told him yes, and he said that I married him for his money, and I said, "No, he married me for mine." My husband got up in his face and told Don that he was so full of shit that his eyes were brown. Then Don left and did not come back. Don had put on a lot of weight. I was the best thing that ever happened to him. He went out with trash, but I wish him well. As I was telling you in the first part of this book, I would stay with him until I freed his wife from him. I went through hell myself too, but now this woman could start her life anew. That's my story, and I am sticking to it, but I do wish her and her children all the best in life.

When Don lied to me about what he was doing on Tuesday night because he was supposed to be at my place by 7 PM, I called and there was no answer. So I called Don's mom, and she told me he had gone to the show with his wife. So I waited until I figured he would be home, and then I called him at 10:30 PM, and he was home so I asked him where he was. He replied that he was sleeping, so I played along with him, and said, "Are you coming over tonight?" Don said yes. So I waited until Don was in my house and sat down, and we talked for about ten minutes, and he continued to tell me that he had fallen asleep and did not hear the phone. Then I was fed up with his lies so I asked him if he wanted to tell me where he really was, and he still said that he was sleeping. I told him that I knew that he had taken his wife to the show, and he got very angry and stood up and again tried to leave because he could not stand being caught in a lie once again. I threw him over the sofa. Don was a compulsive liar and an alcoholic.

He Is a Liar

This was a Friday night. It was about 7 PM again. I called him, and he did not answer his phone, so I called his daughter to see if she had talked to her dad, and she said that he was home because she was talking to him on the other line. She told me to go over and knock on his door. I could hear his television on, but it was very low. It was not hard to hear it because he lived in a rooming house in one room. So I left and parked my car around on the next street and called his daughter and told her that her dad had not answered the door. She told me to go back over there, and she would call him and keep him on the phone. She told me that he was upstairs at his friend's place, which was just catty-cornered from his. I left my car around the corner, and I walked through the deep snow. I arrived at his place, and there was a cab driver at the door, so I said, "Excuse me," and I went up to the second floor. When I got up to his place, I could hear him clearing his throat a lot, and I could hear him talking on the phone upstairs at his friend's place. Don's daughter had told me that she would give me ten minutes and then she would call his place. So when his phone

The Life I Lived With So Called Elvis

was ringing, I was on the landing of the hallway, and I heard him coming down the stairs. I didn't know where to go, so I quickly got against the wall outside of his door, and he could not see me there. So after I knew his feet were on the landing, I popped out and said, "What kind of game are you playing?" He turned as white as a ghost. He had frozen right in his steps, and I said a few choice words and told him that he was not dealing with a full deck, and then I just left. I knew he was not a normal person, but I believe that no matter what they look like or how they dress, everyone deserves a chance because I am a classy lady, and God only knows why I took Don under my wing. He was twelve years younger than I, but the age to me is just a number. It's what is in your heart that counts.

Our First Little Boat Cruise

This is about a boat cruise we went on. It was just for the evening. All "Elvis" would wear was black pants and shirt as well as black shoes. I told him that if he was going on the boat, he would have to wear something different. Don said, "I don't think so," so I told him that I was going by myself.

Days later, he called and said that he had gotten what I had suggested, and I was surprised. I asked him where he had gotten the clothes, and he said, "The Amity." I was stunned that with all his money he would go there. Don said that he always bought his clothes there and that it didn't matter where you bought your clothes. He was as cheap as they come. On Saturday night, we went to go on our boat trip. After the bus was underway, he had a hate on, and I did not know why. But after we were on the boat, he said that I knew a lot of people and would not speak to me the rest of the night. We had two dances, and he had not said a word so when we got home, I told him to grow up, and that did not go over too well. After I was at home having a cup of tea I thought that if that boy dressed like this all the time, it would be nice because he

The Life I Lived With So Called Elvis

looked really good. So from then on, Don started to try wearing different colors and styles, and it kind of stopped him from thinking that he was Elvis all the time. We went to a wedding, and Don dressed up very nicely, and I even loved him more. Now it was 2002, and I still thought of Don a lot. I wish things would have turned out differently. On the cruise, Don wore white pants, a red shirt, and a black jacket. He was a whole different-looking man at the wedding. Don wore black pants, a pink shirt, and a black jacket. What a difference. This started to change him for the better. Everyone was saying that they found a big difference in Don's looks and his dancing. There was, but nothing lasts forever.

How He Was Mean to His Mom

This so-called Elvis was very mean to his mother. She had a bad heart, but he did not help her in any way. All Don gave her was grief. She would walk to the grocery store and back. Don's mom was in no shape to be doing this, so I told her that if she wanted to go for food, I would take her there, and she told me if Don took her she would have to pay her son. She lived all alone in one big room that had her kitchen, bathroom, and sitting room. So some days I would pick her up and bring her to my place. We had tea and talked. All the time she was there, she was afraid to be there because he could walk in at any time. I told his mom that he would never get in unless I wanted him to. So I made his mom a nice lunch and then took her home. She was seventy-nine and in ill health, so I took her home and made sure that there was no one around. She told me that she would like to see her sister before she died. So I told her to tell me when she would like to go and that we would take her to see her. She said that Don wouldn't go for that, and I told her that if I told him to he would do it. She asked if we could go Saturday, and I told her that we would pick her up at ten o'clock. So I asked Don, and he said that it was too far, and I told him that I would drive but that we were taking his car. He did not like it at all. Off we went, and it took us an hour and a half. We arrived, and they had a nice visit. It was nice to see the two of them together. They hugged one another, and they talked and talked. It was nice to see, and I am glad that we took the time to do that for her. Even Don had a good time laughing and talking. We took pictures and had lunch. We left at about five o'clock and got home at seven. Don's mother was very tired so we went in to make sure she would be okay. I told her that we would stay until she fell asleep, and she said okay. She was so glad to have seen her sister. The next time she went for groceries, the poor soul walked all that way with a bad heart. On the way home, she had an attack and went to the hospital. She was in for two weeks and then came home. Her granddaughter was going to stay with her for a day or two, so I told her that if she needed to go to get groceries, we would take her. She said that Don made her pay him ten dollars, and I told her to keep her money and that she did not have to pay him to take her to get things she needed. Well, come Sunday, she called me and said, "Thank you for what you did."

Then Don started a fight over nothing so "Elvis" went to his mom's and took a bottle of vodka even though she does not like him drinking at her place. She called me and told me that he was there but he had stepped out. I said, "Is he giving you a hard time?" She told me that she had to go because he was coming back in. Well, it was not too long before he called me. I was nice to him so that he would not give his mom a hard time. He said that he would call me later, and I said okay. Ten minutes later,

Judith Martin

he called me again, and I told him that I thought that he had better go home and let his mom go to bed. So then everything was cool. His mom called the next day and told me that Don, his wife, and his daughter kept her awake all night. If it was not one of them on the phone, it was the other one. She told me that she fell asleep at the kitchen table with the phone in her hand. She had to go and get food, and no one was around to take her, and so she walked all the way there and all the way back. Needless to say, she ended up in the hospital again and was there for about three weeks. I had gone to see her, and she would not open her eyes at all, but she knew I was there. I think that she did not want to be bothered with her kids, so I told her that I was going to Florida, and she just squeezed my hand, and I told her to please try not to let the kids get to her. I told her that I loved her and that I would see her when I came back. She said okay and that she loved me. I started to cry and left. I came home from Florida late at night, but the first thing in the morning, I called my girlfriend, and she asked me if I knew that Don's mom had passed away. I told her no because I had just gotten in last night from my trip. She told me that the funeral was at ten o'clock. I never knew I could move so fast in my life, but I got there in time, thank God. And that was the end of Elvis, but I still to this day have feelings for him after all that he put me through.

Don Being a Whole Different Person

Don was a different person when he was not around me. His daughter would call me and say that she was calling her dad and ask if I would like to listen. I said, "Why do you want me to listen in?" She said because she was mad at him and that she wanted me to hear how he talked to her when I wasn't around. She had three-way calling, and I knew that it was not the right thing to do, but I said okay. She told me not to say anything no matter what was said. So she called Don and started talking to him. She asked him if he had talked to me today, and he said yes. She asked Don if he loved me, and Don said no. She said to her father that he had been with me for two years and asked how he could say that. Don said all kinds of things that I would not repeat. This was the first time I ever heard Don use the F-word, and it went on and on. Don's daughter was upset with him, and little did I know, she talked to her dad the same way. I am not used to that kind of language. Don was mad at his daughter, so it went on and on, but of course I could not say anything

Judith Martin

or he would know that I was on the line at the same time. I thought I had heard bad language before, but I heard things that I had never heard in my life.

I knew Don could get angry because I had seen him that way, but as far as the so-called Elvis, he had the same kind of mean streak as the real Elvis, thinking he could tell me what to do, but I just told him that it was my place and if he couldn't stand the heat then he knew where the door was and to not let it hit him on the way out. Then he got up in an uproar and just went back to his seat and sat and stared at me.

I know that deep down he still loves me even though he would never admit it. I know it is true. If I wanted to go back with him, he would take me back in a heartbeat. Even though Elvis would, there is no way in hell.

We had a lot of feelings for one another. They were stronger than the still water runs deep. There was a time that Don told me he would be late getting to my place, so I had my friend follow him from work. Even though you love someone, if there is no trust, you have nothing.